I NEVER WANTED

by

Arlene Klein

A COLLECTION OF POEMS
Gentle words to comfort those who mourn the loss of a pet

Arlene Klein
—2014

Illustrations by Ron Klein

Foreword by Betty White

Publisher, DESIGNING POET ™
P.O. Box 18747
Sarasota, Florida 34276
www.designingpoet.com

Arlene Klein
Revised edition of: I NEVER WANTED TO SAY GOODBYE,
first edition, 1995 ISBN 0-9650915-0-3

ISBN 0-9650915-3-8

ISBN 978-0-9650915-3-4

Dedicated to the dogs in my life who have been my life

and

To my grandchildren, Erica, Mindy , Alex and Michael with love

ALSO by ARLENE KLEIN

The Grandfather of Possibilities Inventor-Entrepreneur-Athlete
An Inspirational Biography

ACKNOWLEDGMENTS

My heartfelt thanks to:

My parents who allowed me the companionship and responsibility of pets during my childhood.

My friends in the world of dogs, whose encouragement was the driving force for me to write this book.

My Veterinarians; Dr. William Mekenney, Dr. David Watkins and Dr. Stephanie Lantry for their knowledge, concern and excellent care.

My daughter, Lori Schwartz and my friend and former secretary, and superb "Dog Nanny," Diane Tagliavia, for the care and attention given to the dogs in my absence. They have made it possible for me to work for the welfare of the animals that share our world.

Love and gratitude to my husband, Ron, for his confidence in me. My everlasting gratitude for the support, computer expertise and precious hours he gave to publish this book.

Last, but not least, hugs to my beloved Yorkie, Scout. You taught me patience, the greatest lesson of all. You are the joy of my life!

Arlene Klein

FOREWORD

Dear Friend:

Losing a best buddy is always tough ... no less so if that cherished companion happens to have four legs. But the present pain is a reasonable price to pay weighed against all the happy times of mutual devotion.

These days we are at last able to own up to our grief at the loss of a beloved pet ... and those who don't understand are the poorer for it.

No matter how large or how tiny your friend, the words of Arlene Klein contained herein will apply.

May they bring you comfort.

Love,

Betty White

INTRODUCTION

In an ever-growing impersonal world, the personal relationship with our pets is of significant importance. The dedication and unconditional love that our pets give is beyond compare.

Studies have shown the many benefits to the health and well being of people. The elderly, the sick and the disabled benefit from the companionship of a pet. Laws have been passed that allow pets in nursing homes, hospitals and day-care centers. Service dogs are the eyes, the ears and the hands to many.

All of us who are privileged to share our lives with a companion animal know the joy of having them and the sorrow of losing them. One day, we all must face the dreaded moment when we say goodbye to our beloved friend.

I wrote these poems as a tribute to the dogs that I loved and lost. I hope these gentle words bring comfort to others who mourn the loss of a treasured pet.

Photo by Bernard Kernan

ONCE UPON A PUPPY

Sheer joy was he from the start,
My first little puppy, he warmed my heart.
Like springtime seedlings bursting, my canine family grew.
As time took flight, five more puppies new.

I savored the fun filled hours each day
Of bonding with them and watching them play.
Their gleeful clamor was music to my ears.
Merriment was abound when they were near.

In the lap of luxury my puppies lulled,
Pampered and protected like treasures of gold.
A very special love for them did exist,
For those priceless creatures in my midst.

I prayed for the sweet moments to stay,
But, so swiftly the time seemed to slip away.
My little puppies too soon grew old.
The next chapter of their life would soon unfold.
If only the years could tenfold be
For the little puppies that were a part of me.

Twelve years passed and they began to ail.
Like a dark shadow, silence prevailed.
The house grew still, more hours did they sleep.
All too soon death upon them would creep.
Each passing day I was overcome with fear
That my world would shatter without them here.

I was privileged for the years we shared
Dedicated love. I was always there
for the little puppies that I lived for
      They will be a part of me forevermore.

Photo by Bernard Kernan

A SPECIAL LOVE FOR NERO

Gracefully he gaited around the ring.
So beautiful was he, but no spirit did he bring.
With downcast eyes he looked at me
And I knew then, mine he would be.

Tho he could not speak, his eyes told all
About the people, that to him were cruel.
They revealed the story of neglect endured.
Of a life in a crate, his needs ignored.

He had reached the tender age of four
And deserved to be nurtured, neglected no more.
Nero would have a new life in store;
I would rescue him and love him forevermore.

As the weeks went by, he learned fast
That he had a real home at last.
Like fading shadows, reminders of his past
Vanished. Happiness for him in stone was cast.

He loved to toss his silly toys
And run and play with the other boys.
He would wait as I tended to his needs.
Always grateful for the attention he received,
He thanked me with kisses for my deeds.

He died at twelve and was laid to rest
In the garden where the birds nest.
Where squirrels and cottontails scamper to and fro,
Where daylilies blossom and honeysuckle grow.

A beautiful vision beyond the gate I see
Of Nero with nature's critters, playing happily.
Tho he is gone we are never apart,
Because he lives forever in my heart.

I visit him, when to the garden I go
Each morning at sunrise when gentle breezes blow.
Because I have
                a special love for Nero.

Photo by Bernard Kernan

ODE TO DUSTY

From the moment I held you it was love at first sight,
Your beautiful face, your eyes so bright.
You were my first show dog, so sassy and smart,
Small and mighty and five pounds of heart.
You had many admirers both near and afar,
You were one of a kind, my shining star.

I learned more from you than you did from me.
You introduced me to a world where I never knew I'd be.
The places I've been and the special people I've met
Are all because of you, my precious pet.

You were always like a puppy till the very end.
My beautiful Dusty, my best little friend
You grew older, but never old.
Always a terrier, proud, brave and bold.

And when your final days drew nigh
I could not bear to say goodbye.
But mine was not to question why,
For all God's creatures must one day die.
I had you and lost you, it's a hurt and a sorrow.
I wanted you with me for all my tomorrows.

Memories of you are love, laughter and fun,
Playing and training and watching you run.
The photos, the trophies, the ribbons you won,
Your life was full, my precious one.

Trixie, Tinkie, Buttons and Nero I lost in the past,
I still have wonderful memories that will always last.
My sweet Casey, your life hangs by a hair.
Soon I will have to say goodbye, for that I must prepare.

For RJ, DD and Kody a long and healthy life I pray,
I will love and cherish you and embrace everyday.
Dusty, I miss you more than words can say
And will think of you always for the rest of my days.
You have touched the lives of both dog and man
So much more than most people can.

My passion for all animals is alive and well,
I'm dedicated to their welfare and my story I tell.
Video, articles, Morris Animal Foundation work I do,
My commitment to dogkind is because of you.

Best friends who share our lives are worthy of
Our care, devotion and unconditional love.
We can make a difference, the well being of animals
we can affect
With love and concern, compassion and respect.

"You are part dog," an old friend once said to me.
I politely replied, "Thank you, I certainly agree."
I considered it a compliment and hoped that she could see
If people had dogs' qualities
                    what a wonderful world it would be.

MADELINE CALLED

When first we met she was in her prime,
Smitten with disease and taken before her time.
A woman of talents, jewelry she made.
Creations so fine, not long did they stay
In the case where they were displayed.

The gold Yorkie pin I wore on my lapel,
I lost one day. To the ground it fell
And was missing for months until found,
Like a brilliant gold star sparkling on the ground.

Dusty was so ill and failing rapidly.
Our last day together; the next..God took him from me.
I slipped the red lead on him for his last short walk.
He stopped and stared at the pin like a hawk.

The gold Yorkie pin is now atop the box
That contains Dusty's ashes. The treasures it locks
Of all the reminders of yesterday.
The joyous times that will forever with me stay.

I gaze at his picture on the wall.
All the love and joy that I recall
Are now only memories, because
                            Madeline called.

Photo by Bernard Kernan

Photo by Bernard Kernan

LOVING

The silence of the night is broken with a pant and a roar,
Then a pause, normal breathing and silence once more.
I turn and watch you as you continue to sleep.
Relieved and calm, I begin to weep.

My heart is barely healed from my loss of recent days
And now I must face losing you, in spite of how I pray
That you can be with me just a little longer
To frolic, to play and to become a little stronger.
But I know it's only a dream that I wish could come true,
For I know in reality, it's time to say goodbye to you.

You have struggled with illness for the past three years.
I have held and comforted you and have shed my tears.
My sweet Casey, you have weathered your aches and pains,
Always so stoic, you have never complained.

Again a pant and then a roar,
But this time there is silence no more.
Your breathing is labored, I know now it's true
That the bitter moment has come; I am losing you.

I awake at dawn to kisses on my cheek.
I greet the day and try not to be bleak.
The younger dogs are a reason to smile and be gay.
They bring joy to my life in so many ways.

A symphony of barks and pitter-patters; outside the dogs go
And another day begins; another day to show
How much I love them. My contentment grows
As we play together and toys to them I throw.

Animal is from the Latin word meaning soul.
They are a living, breathing spirit, into whose mind man
cannot stroll.
My dogs are my inspiration, my love and my life.
They have always been my strength in times of strife.

With the animals that share our world we do connect,
A lesson in life on which to reflect.
We are not superior beings, because we can think and speak.
Dogs are compassionate and intelligent and are never weak.
They are honest and loyal and have qualities that many
humans lack.
They can teach man many things and man should give back
Love and respect to
             the purest of God's creatures.

Rest in peace my sweet Casey.

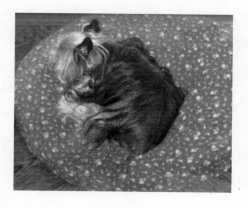

ERICA'S SONG

"MomMom! Dusty and Casey are not old and sick anymore.
They are in heaven. They are happy and they play."
The words I will cling to forevermore
About the little dogs she still looks for.

Her gentle voice trails on, soft as silk.
She takes a bite of a cookie and a sip of milk.
She continues to gaze at the photos on the wall
Of the dogs she loves and their names she calls.
RJ, DD and Kody come and sit at her feet.
She hugs and kisses them and she repeats,
"MomMom! Dusty and Casey are not old and sick anymore.
They are in heaven. They are happy and they play."

Words so profound from one so small,
One so young with no experience at all
Except the love and kindness she gives
To the animals she knows, who with me live.

A myriad of visions before my eyes pass
Of years shared with the dogs that flew by so fast.
The last haunting memory that I try to erase
Of the stare in their eyes, the look on their face.
At last, those thoughts I can finally replace
With pleasant dreams of them in a faraway place.

Summer and autumn quickly passed by,
The cold winter is here and spring draws nigh.
Time has healed the pain and now I clearly see
The dogs where Erica wants them to be.
The genuine love of a child only three,
She takes my hand and utters to me,
"MomMom! Dusty and Casey are not old and sick anymore.
They are in heaven. They are happy and they play."

MINDY'S NEW WORLD

Will she love them as I do,
These furry little creatures to her so new?
I introduce them one by one.
She does not cry, she is not stunned.

As they chase around her on the floor,
She watches to see what's in store.
Only four months old, she wants to explore.
Nothing they do does she ignore.

Too young to hate, too young to fear,
Her fascination grows when they are near.
With a tiny, dimpled, outstretched hand
She strokes their fur to feel each strand.

She casts her eyes upon their red bows of lace,
While ever so gently RJ licks her face.
The other dogs wait; Kody obediently in place
With DD, each awaiting their fond embrace.

The majesty of the moment in my heart I'll hold,
A memory to cherish when someday I'm old.
Mindy smiles and begins to coo.
Yes,
       she will love them as I do.

HOW MANY SUNSETS

They wait. They watch and barely utter a sound,
Yearning to be free from shelters bound.
Will a proper home for them soon be found?
On page after page in newsletters that arrive
Are the pitiful faces of those who won't survive.

Neglected and abused, cast aside because no one cared.
Will someone adopt them? Will their lives be spared?
All of them have so much potential
To establish their worth, to be someone special.

Or will they be victims who needlessly die,
Robbed of their years, their happiness denied?
How many sunsets before they are no longer here?
Will anyone mourn them or shed a tear?

They are gone. No longer do they wait.
My hope, as they rest beyond heavens gate,
Is that every man we can educate
That animals are a gift from God above,

Given to us to cherish and love.

PAWPRINTS ON MY HEART

Once it was a happy canine family of six.
A time of joy, wags and licks.

Celebrate their days, too soon they part.
One day, they left pawprints on my heart.
I know that time is like fine sand.
It so quickly slips thru our hand.

To Nero, Dusty and Casey I said goodbye.
Their days were numbered, soon they would die.
They left a hole in my heart,
When from my world they had to depart.

RJ, DD and Kody were the remaining three.
They were young and healthy and still with me.
I tasted the beauty of every moment with them.
They brought me happiness, my furry gems.

All so special in their own unique way.
DD, Dusty's daughter; petite and sassy I would say.
RJ, her brother; adorable, with the heart of a lion,
Somewhat unpredictable, but a ray of sunshine.
And my little Kody, such a "babylike" boy,
His beautiful blue coat and long eyelashes,
To merely look at him was a joy.

It was a time of laughter and fun.
Happy pups played and lulled in the sun.
They were traveling dogs, escorting us everywhere.
They loved the attention, when all would stare
At the parade of three pooches who had such flare,
So well behaved, something quite rare.

I savored every precious day, because I knew their time would come.
As those before them, they would succumb.
Too soon they left me and I felt such pain,
But the warm memories of them will always remain.
The house was quiet, no fur at my feet.
There was an empty feeling, life was incomplete.

An angel entered; a dog beyond belief.
Scout The Yorkie would help heal the grief.
He came into my life at the age of five
And became my soulmate. I felt alive!
He grabbed at my heart and never let go.
The essence of joy, he made me glow.

So sweet, beautiful and extremely smart,
He's my little prince and we're never apart.
Oh, the things he's done and the places he's been.
He loves everyone and they love him.

Now he is beginning to grow old.
The winter of his life is about to unfold.
Although he still plays like a pup, he's twelve.
I dare not think about it or dare to delve.

I embrace every magical moment we share,
He's the center of my universe, of this I'm aware.
And when he crosses over, I know the pain I'll bear.
But he'll live in my heart forever, this I swear.

Make every day count, because time goes by fast.
Dogs' lives are short and too soon they pass.
Their life is a journey and they love the ride
With you, the master at their side.

Celebrate their days, too soon they part.
One day, they will leave pawprints on your heart.
Remember,
        time is like find sand. It quickly slips through your hand.

ABOUT THE AUTHOR

ARLENE KLEIN has had a love affair with animals forever. Her passion for companion animals and her respect for all living creatures grew, as did her concern for the health and welfare of the animals that share our world.

Her dogs have always been valued members of her family and she is dedicated to their well-being. All of her dogs were formally obedience trained. She has exhibited in Breed Conformation since 1982, owner handling her first show dog to his American Championship.

Deeply concerned for the millions of animals that are neglected, abused, lost and abandoned, she produced a video on responsible pet ownership. A DAY IN THE LIFE of A DOG gained national acclaim. In 1991 it was nominated for a Dog Writers' Association of America Maxwell Award.

She has served on the Board of Trustees of MORRIS ANIMAL FOUNDATION since 1991. She served on the Board of Directors of THE HUMANE SOCIETY OF SARASOTA COUNTY and SOUTHEASTERN GUIDE DOGS.

She is a member of THE LATHAM FOUNDATION, DOG WRITERS' ASSOCIATION OF AMERICA, YORKSHIRE TERRIER CLUB OF AMERICA and many animal-related organizations.

She has written articles about the Human/Animal Bond for national publications.

She is the creator and designer of DESIGNING POET'S DOGGIE NOTE CARDS.

She and her husband live in Sarasota, Florida with their beloved Yorkshire Terrier, SCOUT.

Photo by Cherry Hill Studios

www.MorrisAnimalFoundation.org

A PORTION OF THE PROCEEDS IS DONATED TO MORRIS ANIMAL FOUNDATION FOR CANINE HEALTH STUDIES